Cover Design: Suzanne Tinker-Warn

—Dick Warn—

Books written by Dick Warn:

The Miracle Minute
52 One Minute Guides to Practical Wisdom
Published January, 2006

More Miracle Minutes
52 One Minute Guides to Practical Wisdom
Published August, 2007

Mystical Mentor
Breaking through Barriers – Finding Peace of Mind
Fourth Quarter, 2007

—More Miracle Minutes—

More Miracle Minutes

52 One Minute Guides to Practical Wisdom

Dick Warn

Order this book online at www.trafford.com/07-0951
or email orders@trafford.com

Most Trafford titles are also available at major online book retailers.

© Copyright 2007 Dick Warn.

All rights reserved. No part of this publication may be reproduced, stored in a retrieval system, or transmitted, in any form or by any means, electronic, mechanical, photocopying, recording, or otherwise, without the written prior permission of the author.

Note for Librarians: A cataloguing record for this book is available from Library and Archives Canada at www.collectionscanada.ca/amicus/index-e.html

Printed in Victoria, BC, Canada.

ISBN: 978-1-4251-2764-0

We at Trafford believe that it is the responsibility of us all, as both individuals and corporations, to make choices that are environmentally and socially sound. You, in turn, are supporting this responsible conduct each time you purchase a Trafford book, or make use of our publishing services. To find out how you are helping, please visit www.trafford.com/responsiblepublishing.html

Our mission is to efficiently provide the world's finest, most comprehensive book publishing service, enabling every author to experience success. To find out how to publish your book, your way, and have it available worldwide, visit us online at www.trafford.com/10510

www.trafford.com

North America & international
toll-free: 1 888 232 4444 (USA & Canada)
phone: 250 383 6864 ♦ fax: 250 383 6804
email: info@trafford.com

The United Kingdom & Europe
phone: +44 (0)1865 722 113 ♦ local rate: 0845 230 9701
facsimile: +44 (0)1865 722 868 ♦ email: info.uk@trafford.com

10 9 8 7 6 5 4 3 2

— *More Miracle Minutes* —

A Miracle Minute is any moment in time when we see something in a new light and it changes us, allowing us to achieve more than we ever have before.

Some Miracle Minutes will inspire us to laugh; others will poke holes in myths, and a few will remind us of powerful principles we've forgotten.

Driven by our desires, guided by our beliefs, and limited by our fears, we wander through a classroom called life. By questioning, searching and reading, we gain new understandings and shafts of light break through.

May your days make room for reading, may your hands have plenty to do, and may your journey unfold with breathtaking breakthroughs.

Dick Warn

Tualatin, Oregon USA

—Dick Warn—

—*More Miracle Minutes*—

Praise for Book 1: First 52 Miracle Minutes

"I found each concept in your book to touch my life, whether it be personal, professional or both. The book brought me a sense of peace and reflection."

Paulette Talbot, Supervisor
Learning & Organizational Development
PEMCO Financial Services
Seattle, Washington USA

"Dick Warn gives us practical and profound wisdom that always seems to hit the spot. I work with recovering drug addicts and they can sniff malarkey a mile away. They like "The Miracle Minute" because it moves us past nice sounding words to truths that transform."

Bill Russell, Executive Director
Union Gospel Mission
Portland, Oregon USA

"Your Miracle Minutes have caused me to be very thankful for the powerful insights you share."

Juan Marcos
Clear Channel Radio
Riverside, California USA

—*Dick Warn*—

"*Dick, you have the best way to put things.*"

Sonia Sue Beckwith
Woodland, Washington USA

"*Neil and I read a bit of "The Miracle Minute" each evening. Lots of great insights and reinforcements of the good aspects of life.*"

Kimberly Morey, Marketing Manager
Kauai, Hawaii USA

"*I'm in outside sales and when I finished reading it I was ready to take on the planet. This book gives you simple uplifting lessons that everyone encounters each day in language that we can all relate to. I am keeping this book close and have made a personal commitment to pick it up and read from it every day. I love this book!*"

Lynda Lemke, Account Executive
KZSW Television
Temecula, California USA

"*Dick, I read one of your Miracle Minutes today in front of 40 marketers. It was easy. The results were awesome.*"

Mac Soderquist, Sales Director
Club 120 Resorts & International Tree Club
Lake Oswego, Oregon USA

— *More Miracle Minutes* —

"Dick, your Miracle Minutes have provided insights into unhealthy doubts hovering in my mind. Now I am driven to do what needs to be done."

Pasquale Mansi, Managing Director
Ufficio Limited
Ashwell, Herts, Great Britain

"The Miracle Minutes do make a difference."

Sherman A. Rainge
International Customer Development Director
Nestle Waters Management and Technology
France

"I have to tell you Dick, I read your book out loud to Paul (my husband) on our way home from Northern California — the whole thing. It's such a quick read and so full of wisdom. I let Nathan (my son) read it, too. What inspiring reading. You truly are a gifted writer."

Pat Kalpakoff
Fresno, California USA

—*Dick Warn*—

—More Miracle Minutes—

Introduction

If you have read "The Miracle Minute – Book 1" some of this is a repeat.

Book publishers claim that 90% percent of the books sold are purchased by less than three 3% of the people.

What does that mean? It means that you—if you purchased this book, and also you—if you received this as a gift—are either in the top 3%, or thinking about being there.

The greatest material gift anyone can give themselves or anyone else is a life-enhancing book. The wisest thoughts, the most powerful methods, and the universal truths enabling peace of mind exist in print.

It is not the words that make a difference, but the meaning behind the words. If you are searching for more practical meanings—this book is filled with views that may be new to you.

—*Dick Warn*—

Each Miracle Minute can be read in less than 60 seconds, and each should be followed by questions such as, "What did Dick Warn mean? What does this mean to me? And, what—if anything—might I or we do differently?"

Will every Miracle Minute be a perfect fit for you? Hardly! Some will miss the mark, others will spark awesome thought, and a few will alter your life forever. One old truth, newly understood—is worth more than the price of any book.

Having spent most of my life trying to help others gain valuable insights, I have discovered that simple thought pieces like The Miracle Minute work much better than recorded messages and video. And, in training sessions, a Miracle Minute allows facilitators to be highly effective—without preparation.

Whether we like it or not, we are all riding together on Space-ship Earth and there is no way to change planets. The very best we can do is to learn from the lessons we have been given and, if we are willing, we can become miracle workers in the lives of others.

— *More Miracle Minutes* —

When we help others see their deep-seated beliefs in a new light—changes and occasional miracles do occur. Our thinker—that thing which we call our mind—is our creator.

A few readers rush right through these *52 Guides to Practical Wisdom* as if the book was a "happy meal" and they need to find the toy. Readers can do that, but that isn't the best way to go.

To find the "toys"—the simple insights that make a difference, read one chapter at a time and think about what's been shared. It is the thought you bring to these words that give them power.

May your journey through life be filled with new adventures, more joy, and unexpected blessings.

Dick Warn

www.TheMiracleMinute.com

—Dick Warn—

—*More Miracle Minutes*—

Author's Acknowledgements

No author stands alone.

In this case, 11 people were directly involved in the creation and the success of *The Miracle Minute* series. Had the radio versions not been successful, the book versions would not have been written.

Those individuals playing major roles:

Original Idea –

> **Bill Waddingham,** President
> Excite 1 Corporation
> Lytle Creek, California USA

Air Time and Production Resources –

> **Bob Ridzak,** General Manager
> Clear Channel Radio
> Riverside, California USA

Original Pilot Recordings –

> **Matt Jones,** Engineer
> Clear Channel Radio
> Portland, Oregon USA

—Dick Warn—

Creation of the Music Bed —
Kevin Lamb and Marie Waddingham
Excite 1 Corporation
Lytle Creek, California USA

Final Radio Spots Editing —
Kevin Lamb

On-Air Programming of the spots —
Bill Georgi, Program Director
Clear Channel Radio
Riverside, California USA

Original Idea for the Books —
Bonnie Goulding, Production Assistant
KNMT-TV 24
Portland, Oregon USA

Cover Designs for all of the Books —
Suzanne Tinker-Warn, Graphic Designer
Frog Pond Enterprises, Inc.
Tualatin, Oregon USA

Editing Services for all of the Books —
Mari Kennedy
Editing Professionals
Portland, Oregon USA

Publishing of the Books —
Trafford Publishing
Victoria, British Columbia, Canada

In addition to the firms, friends and people I have just mentioned, there are many others who have played a role in who I have become, what I believe and what I write. I thank everyone who has ever touched me in anyway. I am grateful for who I have become.

There were times when I didn't feel grateful. Lonely and depressing nights when I considered dropping out—as if I were in school. Yet I didn't. In spite of my regrets, fears and guilt, I crawled back up and took another swing at life.

Recently someone asked, "How did you learn so much?" And I simply replied, "By falling down so often."

I have never learned that much from winning. My greatest discoveries have always resulted from my deepest despairs and loneliest days.

We should never be afraid of losing or falling down—it is how we learn.

Thank you for being here.

—*Dick Warn*—

—*More Miracle Minutes*—

—Miracle Minutes in Book 2—

1 — Frustration Is Your Friend
2 — Making Everything Easier
3 — Perfectionism Is Self-Abuse
4 — Fear Is a Closed Door
5 — Defining Moments Demand Action
6 — Examples of Sound Character Needed
7 — What Is A Real Friend?
8 — Key to Growth
9 — Dare to Be More Daring
10 — Four Simple Truths
11 — Explaining Ethics to a Teenager
12 — Key to Happiness
13 — Our Keys to Freedom
14 — Clues to Your Success
15 — Why Wait?
16 — Dealing With Insults and Grudges

17 —   The Art of Saying NO

18 —   Slow Down Your Aging

19 —   When Feeling Down

20 —   Why Belong to a Trade Association?

21 —   Students and Music

22 —   It's All About Choices

23 —   The Wisest Way to Learn

24 —   Stay Close To Your Best People

25 —   At-Bats, Hits, and Misses

26 —   Worry and Stress—A Nation's Killers

27 —   Putting Our World Together

28 —   Follow-Through

29 —   Less Stressful Living

30 —   Ten Two-Letter Words

31 —   Persistent Endless Trying

32 —   What Words Will You Choose?

33 —   We *CAN* Reinvent Ourselves

34 —   Having A Bird's-Eye View

35 —   Inch by Inch

— *More Miracle Minutes* —

36 —   The Price of Bad Advice

37 —   Is It Tiger's Talent—or Luck?

38 —   The Substance-Abuse Lie

39 —   When a Leaf Falls

40 —   A Pivotal Key

41 —   Who Do You Hang With?

42 —   Trust Your Intuitive Feelings

43 —   Fight-or-Flight Response

44 —   Three Myths About Success

45 —   Three Myths About Money

46 —   What It Means to Be Truly Alive

47 —   Making Enough Changes?

48 —   Fran Tarkenton Said

49 —   Earl Nightingale's Strangest Secret

50 —   Two Signs of Meaningful Maturity

51 —   The Keys to Getting

52 —   Harry S. Truman Said

       Closing Comments

       More About Dick Warn

—Dick Warn—

ONE

Ω

Frustration Is Your Friend

You were born with a wide-open mind and the ability to create an awesome life. So why are so many people dragging themselves through miserable messes? Because they were taught to play it safe, never take risks, and were rewarded with gold stars for memorizing what others claim. This process produces non-risk-taking miserable people.

As American judge, James F. Byrnes, once said, *"Too many people are thinking of security instead of opportunity. They seem more afraid of life than death."*

—Dick Warn—

Security-driven non-risk-takers are committing suicide on the installment plan. To be fully alive, we need to be stretching for something we want, trying things we have never done, and making enough mistakes to discover our strengths and weaknesses.

Our Maker didn't make any losers. Frustration is Nature's way of telling us that we can do much better.

If you are questioning your abilities and feeling frustrated, now is the time to stretch.

TWO

Ω

Making Everything Easier

Some mornings you may awaken with a desire to take on the world. Other mornings you may want to just roll over.

A preacher once asked an old Indian chief, *"How's it going?"*

The chief replied, *"Ever since you asked me to give my heart to God a black dog and a white dog have been fighting in my mind."*

—*Dick Warn*—

The preacher asked, *"Which one wins?"* And the old chief replied, *"The one that I feed."*

If you would like to find a proven way to make life easier, please try this: Each morning, before starting your day, read an uplifting book for at least 20 minutes, and then spend 10 minutes giving thanks—thanks for what you have, the people you care about, and the freedom you have to improve your life. Then, right before going to sleep at night, repeat the process.

Once you begin this method of feeding your mind you will find something that only the wisest people know. The most rewarding way to go through life is with an uplifted spirit and an Attitude of Gratitude. It makes everything in life so much easier.

THREE

Ω

Perfectionism Is Self-Abuse

Danny Kaye, American entertainer, said, *"Life is a great big canvas; throw all the paint on it you can."*

Carl Jung, Swiss psychologist, said, *"There is no light without shadow, and no psychic wholeness without imperfection. To round itself out, life calls not for perfection, but for completeness."*

Where I have erred in the past is in believing I had to be perfect. Minor flaws looked like mountains, and I spent restless nights worrying about people's opinions. Races I could have won I didn't even enter.

—Dick Warn—

Why did I allow people's opinions to control my decisions? Why did I beat myself down and shoot myself in the foot? I was so busy counting my flaws that I lost sight of the big picture.

In the big picture, everyone has unfulfilled desires, strengths and weaknesses. Everyone gets hit with opinions, and everyone makes mistakes.

It's like a minefield out there. To reach your desires you've got to step over a whole lot of stuff. To be complete, you've got to throw all of your paint.

Please remember two things that Anne W. Schaef said, *"It is possible to be different and still be all right."* And, *"Perfectionism is self-abuse of the highest order."*

FOUR

Ω

Fear Is a Closed Door

Leo Buscaglia, American author, said, *"We all fear what we don't know—it's natural."* This is the reason many authors have said that knowledge is power.

Fear prevents people from discovering their talents, and fear destroys careers, marriages, and other relationships before they even begin.

Henry Ford, founder of Ford Motor Company, said, *"One of the greatest discoveries a man makes, one of his greatest surprises, is to find that he can do what he was afraid he couldn't do."*

—Dick Warn—

None of us knows what we can do until we push ourselves to face our fears. As you already know, fear is a natural aspect of life, and failing to make something work is nature's way of telling us to find another way.

Marilyn Ferguson, American author, said, *"Fear is a question: What are you afraid of, and why? Just as the seed of health is an illness, because illness contains information, our fears are a treasure house of self-knowledge if we explore them."*

Fear is a closed door—one that should be opened.

FIVE

Ω

Defining Moments Demand Action

The American movie, "Tin Cup," shared a powerful point: *"When a defining moment arrives, you can do one of two things. Define the moment, or let the moment define you."*

Abraham Lincoln said, *"Most folks are about as happy as they make up their minds to be."*

Have you noticed what happens when you make up your mind? Once we are truly clear about something we can quit smoking, quit drinking, or walk away from unhealthy situations. How do I know? I've done all three.

—Dick Warn—

For me, the hardest part was making up my mind. What helped was making two lists: "Reasons For," and "Reasons Against." Seeing reasons in writing makes decisions easier.

Where I've gotten in over my head and have been really dumb is in walking the fence. Viktor Frankl, author of *Man's Search for Meaning*, said, "*A human being is a deciding being.*"

We were created to be creative and make decisions.

We have the ability to live rich, rewarding lives, provided we have the courage to act when our defining moments arrive.

SIX

Ω

Examples of Sound Character Needed

Government is blamed for almost everything. Yet, as Canadian jurist and author Thomas C. Haliburton said, *"The happiness of every country depends upon the character of its people, rather than the form of its government."*

Sound character demands an awareness of life's principles, a willingness to do what's right, and the courage to fight for things that matter. Character determines the quality of our life.

Some people, believing life is better elsewhere, move. Yet, wherever they go, they take themselves

—Dick Warn—

with them. As Ralph Waldo Emerson said, *"No change of circumstances can repair a defect of character."*

And, an old proverb states, *"If an ass goes traveling—it will not come home a horse."*

With character being the driving force behind everyone's life, we should remind ourselves of the messages young minds are receiving. Not all movies, games and news stories are driving home healthy messages.

When given the chance, please set an example by doing what you know is right within your own heart. As playwright Oliver Goldsmith said, *"We can preach a better sermon with our life than with our lips."*

SEVEN

Ω

What Is A Real Friend?

To become the very best that we can be we need others to supply encouragement and to point out our flaws that we can't see. Henry Van Dyke, American poet, said, *"In the progress of personality, first comes a declaration of independence, then recognition of interdependence."*

Of all possible relationships, the most rewarding is with a real friend. So what is a real friend?

Walter Winchell, American journalist, said, *"A real friend is one who walks in when the rest of the world walks out."*

—Dick Warn—

British novelist, Edward G. Bulwer-Lytton, said, *"One of the surest evidences of friendship that one individual can display to another is telling him gently of a fault. If any other can excel it, it is listening to such a disclosure with gratitude, and amending the error."*

And British playwright John Gay said, *"An open foe may prove a curse, but a pretended friend is worse."*

In your dealings with others, please remember, real friends' help you grow.

EIGHT

Ω

Key to Growth

A news reporter once asked the devil, *"What is your most powerful weapon?"* And the devil replied, *"It is the wedge of doubt I drive into the human mind."*

Wilma Rudolph, American athlete, said, *"It doesn't matter what you're trying to accomplish. It's all a matter of discipline. I was determined to discover what life held for me beyond the inner-city streets."*

To go beyond where you have been, self-discipline isn't optional. You walk through minefields of myths daily, and two major killers of dreams are doubt and low self-esteem.

—Dick Warn—

What can be done? You can read books about the lives of great people—where they began, what they found, and what they believed.

Belief is the fabric of your being. On some level you know you can do more with your life than you're doing—and you truly can. The key is in finding out how.

Stories of great people point the way.

NINE

Ω

Dare to Be More Daring

Thomas J. Watson, founder of IBM, said, *"Within us all there are wells of thought and dynamos of energy which are not suspected until emergencies arise. Then oftentimes we find that it is comparatively simple to double or triple our former capacities and to amaze ourselves by the results achieved."*

And, Heart Warrior Chosa said, *"In the darkest hours the soul is replenished and given strength to continue and endure."*

Both Watson and Chosa pushed themselves hard enough and long enough to discover cosmic powers

— *Dick Warn* —

helping them when they faced and fought adversity. Most people never discover their strengths because they say, *"I can't"*—without even trying.

A safe way to truly live doesn't exist.

The easy way is not really easy. It's dreadfully boring.

Your talents are many, your days are numbered, and daily life is a gamble.

The best bets you will ever have are betting on yourself.

Don't say *"no"* to life. Say *"yes"* by being more daring.

TEN

Ω

Four Simple Truths

During your days and nights of sharing and caring, please remember Four Simple Truths:

1. We are all riding through space on the same planet. Spaceship Earth is not anyone's to own—it is everyone's to share.

2. We are not free to do as we please. Universal truths and natural laws exist—and they cannot be altered with discretional ethics, political babble or religious misconceptions.

—*Dick Warn*—

3. Peace on Earth is beyond reach, as long as anyone on this planet believes in killing other people to get their way.

4. Killing and other acts of insanity are driven by fear or greed.

The true enemies of global peace are ignorance and greed.

At every opportunity, please remind family and friends of something Frank Borman, American astronaut, once said, "*When you're finally up on the moon, looking back at the Earth, all these differences and nationalistic traits are pretty well going to blend, and you're going to get the concept that maybe this is really one world, and wonder why the hell can't we learn to live together like decent people?*"

ELEVEN

Ω

Explaining Ethics to a Teenager

One afternoon a teenager asked, *"What does 'ethics' mean?"*

And I replied, *"It means doing the right thing, whether or not anyone is watching."*

The young man replied, *"How can I tell when something is right?"*

I said, *"Any action is right when it is in harmony with good—and good is anything that sustains life and makes it*

—Dick Warn—

better. A good deed is something that blesses both the giver and the receiver."

Then the young man asked, *"How does the giver get blessed?"*

My reply, *"When you do right—and you know it is right—you add substance to your self-confidence and your self-esteem, and your inner being grows infinitely stronger.*

"People who take advantage of others undermine their self-esteem, lose confidence, and their inner being is weakened."

As Albert Schweitzer said, *"Ethics is the activity of man directed to secure the inner perfection of his own personality."*

TWELVE

Ω

Key to Happiness

Do possessions create happiness? If so, people with the most toys would be the happiest. But this isn't the case.

Henry Drummond wrote, *"There is no happiness in having or getting, but only in giving."*

And, Albert Schweitzer said to a young audience, *"The only ones among you who will ever be really happy are those of you who find ways to be of service to others."*

—*Dick Warn*—

"Service above self" is not a new idea. Rotary International has been stating this for years, and this powerful principle is based on a timeless truth, *"What you do to another you have done to yourself."*

Possessions are nice, but they cannot deliver Life's greater rewards, such as peace of mind, true friends, happiness, love and joy. These rewards must be earned, and they require self-honesty, self-discipline, spiritual awareness, ethics, empathy, compassion, and a willingness to help make this world a better place for everyone.

Self-centered takers may eat better, yet compassionate givers sleep better.

THIRTEEN

Ω

Our Keys to Freedom

Max Depree said, *"We cannot become what we need to be, remaining what we are."*

And, Anthony Robbins said, *"When people ask me what really changed my life, I tell them that absolutely the most important thing was changing what I demanded of myself."*

None of the rules in life are new. If you want more than you've found, set your sights, raise the bar, and commit to making yourself change.

Change isn't easy. As Gail Sheehy said, *"All changes, even the most longed for, have their melancholy; for what we leave behind is a part of ourselves; we must die to one*

—*Dick Warn*—

life before we can enter into another."

As Norman Mailer said, *"Every moment of one's existence one is growing into more or retreating into less."*

Growth results from facing our fears and doing what needs to be done. It is the inner person that needs to grow. Our willingness to change contains our keys to freedom.

FOURTEEN

Ω

Clues to Your Success

Most of my life I believed that success was winning races, climbing ladders, and acquiring money—so I aimed for the top. The sales races I won I've now forgotten, the gold watch I was given is lost, and the excess funds I'd accumulated allowed me to relax and party. As someone said, *"The road to success is lined with tempting parking spaces."*

Many people believe in staying busy; yet, as Henry David Thoreau, American poet, said, *"It is not enough to be busy. So are the ants. The real question is, 'What are we busy about?'"*

—Dick Warn—

To achieve success, the kind that includes high self-esteem and peace of mind, we must serve the needs of others while applying the Golden Rule—not part of the time, but all of the time.

Erma Bombeck, American humorist, gave us a clue when she said, *"Don't confuse fame with success. Madonna is one; Helen Keller is the other."*

And Zig Ziglar, American motivational speaker, shared another clue when he said, *"You can have anything in the world you want if you'll just help enough other people get what they want."*

FIFTEEN

Ω

Why Wait?

Dr. Robert Anthony, American motivational speaker said, *"There will always be reasons to wait. Truth is, there are only two things in life...reasons and results, and the reasons don't count."*

Why do so many people put off so much when they could be fully alive? Some reasons: The hope that someone else will make them happy, the fear of being wrong, and waiting for signs or better times.

When you need additional facts, dive in. Happiness is the reward we get for pushing ourselves farther than we've ever gone. And, always intending to

—*Dick Warn*—

open books and improve, yet never finding the time is not living—it's dying.

Remember what Haile Selassie once said, "Throughout history, it has been the inaction of those who could have acted; the indifference of those who should have known better; and the silence of the voice of justice when it mattered most that has made it possible for evil to triumph."

Perhaps, in the grand scheme of things, our greatest evil is in not becoming the person we could have been.

SIXTEEN

Ω

Dealing With Insults and Grudges

No matter what we do with our days rude people will cross our paths, and what we need to be mindful of is our reactions.

Everyone has off days, and some are dealing with miserable situations. So, we are going to be hit with insults. One powerful way to deal with them is to detach, forgive and release.

Detachment is the art of not reacting, knowing that the other person isn't at peace with themselves. If they were, they wouldn't be barking and biting.

— *Dick Warn* —

To forgive is not a sign of weakness. As Edwin Chapin said, *"Never does the human soul appear as strong and noble as when it forgoes revenge and dares to forgive."*

Revenge is the need to get even, and holding a grudge is the need to carry bad feelings. Both of these are really heavy burdens. As Buddy Hackett once said, *"I never carry a grudge. You know why? While I'm carrying a grudge, they're out dancing."*

Your key, and mine, to dancing more was shared by Paul Boese, who said, *"Forgiveness does not change the past, but it does enlarge the future."*

SEVENTEEN

Ω

The Art of Saying NO

The last time I made telephone calls seeking volunteers, five out of 10 who said they would help did not show. Why?

About the time children begin potty training, most parents begin working on the child's need to please others. Reinforced with years of *"What other people might think"* lectures, the typical adult's need to be pleasing overrides logic and common sense.

Logic proves that meeting planners need to know what's happening, and that people who make final plans are better off with a *"NO"* than a *"NO SHOW."*

—Dick Warn—

Pleasing is not always helpful, nor is pleasing always respectful. To gain respect, people must say what they mean and mean what they say.

The next time you are asked to do something that you really don't want to do, consider using these words: *"Thank you for asking. I have already made a commitment. I wish you well."*

If any caller is brash enough to ask about your commitment, simply reply, *"It's a personal matter."*

What you do with *"your"* time is personal. And, it is far better to say *"NO"* upfront than deal with the ripple effects of telling lies.

EIGHTEEN

Ω

Slow Down Your Aging

Not everyone is born with the ability to pole vault, play the piccolo or sing in a choir. Yet, everyone arrives with a very powerful mind and eventually develops attitudes about aging.

Aging is a strange process. At 40 some people are used up and mentally dead. Others are still happy campers going strong at 80.

Dorothea Kent, American film actress, once shared, "A man 90 years old was asked to what he attributed his longevity. 'I reckon,' he said, with a twinkle is his eye, 'it

—Dick Warn—

is because most nights I went to bed and slept when others sat up and worried.'"

Individuals who focus on every grey hair and wrinkle, and worry about those they have found, speed up their aging. But those who remain focused on their goals and service to others slow down the process by finding happiness.

The key for you and me is to so occupy our minds with worthy projects that we don't have time to worry about aging. As Sophia Loren, another American actress, said, *"There is a fountain of youth: it is your mind, your talents, the creativity you bring to your life and the lives of the people you love. When you learn to tap into this source, you will truly have defeated age."*

And please remember what Leroy "Satchel" Page, American baseball legend, said, *"Age is a question of mind over matter. If you don't mind—age don't matter."*

NINETEEN

Ω

When Feeling Down

Some days we're flying high, hitting on all cylinders and connecting with everything. Other days the misses take over and we feel down. The next time you're off your game, please consider:

1. Attempts to uncover *"why"* we're off only lead to confusion and deeper depression. So, when the worrisome side of you wants to play in the garbage, don't even go there.

2. Know that you *"can"* do better, and that your mind will find the way when you clearly consider what these people have said:

— *Dick Warn* —

Katharine Hepburn, American actress, said, *"If you want to change, you're the one who has got to change. It's as simple as that, isn't it?"*

Henry Miller, American author, *"We create our fate every day—by our own behavior."*

Franklin D. Roosevelt, 32nd American President, said, *"The only limit to our realization of tomorrow will be our doubts of today. Let us move forward with strong and active faith."*

Tehyi Hsieh, American author, said, *"Action removes the doubts that theory cannot solve."*

No matter what causes us to falter, constructive action is the cure.

TWENTY

Ω

Why Belong to a Trade Association?

Three months ago a friend, buried in problems, decided to withdraw from a trade association. Wanting to help him, I asked, *"In respect to your success, what is the difference between 'efficient' and 'effective'?"*

When he didn't respond, I said, *"'Efficient' is doing the task at hand extremely well. And, 'effective' is doing the right tasks. If you want to grow, the most effective methods can be found by listening to the seasoned old souls who have fought their battles, paid their dues, and achieved success. Rather than walk away from that association, dive in and build a network of experienced people who can help you."*

—*Dick Warn*—

Three months later, when I asked this man how things were going, he said, "*Thanks to you, my most pressing problems can be solved over the phone. We are doing well, and my firm's greatest assets are now the relationships I have within that association—the one I was going to leave.*"

As Daniel Webster said, "*There are many objects of great value which cannot be attained by unconnected individuals, but must be attained, if attained at all, by association.*"

TWENTY-ONE

Ω

Students and Music

In a 1991 U.S. Department of Labor study on creative thinking, invention, self-esteem and imagination, schools were encouraged to "teach the skills learned in music." What things might young musicians discover?

Young musicians would discover that mistakes are natural events in the process of learning. And, they would learn to deal with their mistakes.

—Dick Warn—

Young musicians would discover that an exact set of laws governs your results. That melody and harmony can only be achieved by following the laws.

Young musicians would discover the benefits of teamwork.

And the most driven students would discover the benefits of competition. Competition inspires musicians to work harder and practice longer.

In the world of music there is no place to hide. What you do is heard by everyone, and in terms of Life Sciences—those skills needed to become highly effective—learning to play musical instruments does more to prepare students for real life than any other *"classroom"* subject taught.

Competitive sports are not far behind.

More information on students and music is available at: www.amc-music.org.

TWENTY-TWO

Ω

It's All About Choices

Like spiders weaving their webs, we are also weaving webs of our own with the choices we make.

What causes problems for most people? Two of the biggest causes are fear of failure, and fear of what someone else might think. Like scarecrows in an empty corn field, these fears are trying to fool us. They want us to believe they have power when, in fact, the only power they have is what we give them.

To move forward in life and grow we've got to try things we've never done. This will cause us to fail.

—*Dick Warn*—

So what? Failure isn't failure until we give up. And, all we have to work with is other people's opinions, until we test something ourselves.

The three pivot points that determine the strength of your being are the beliefs you hold of yourself, the truths that you have tested, and the risks you are willing to take at every crossroad.

A rich rewarding life isn't a gift that anyone can give us. It results from all of the little decisions you make along the way and your willingness to stand firm on what you have proven.

Opinions cannot build a backbone.

—More Miracle Minutes—

TWENTY-THREE

Ω

The Wisest Way to Learn

In the game of business, coasting cannot build strength, cutting corners creates problems, and the easiest paths often lead to failure. What, then, is the most powerful way to learn?

If knowledge is power and experience is the best teacher, then the fastest way to get smarter is by asking for the most difficult tasks. When you master the difficult, without bragging or complaining, you gain valuable insights.

—Dick Warn—

What do the wisest people know? They know that true security comes from within—from what a person has learned and proven they can do.

Wise people know that true happiness comes from facing fears, solving problems, and adding value to other people's lives.

Life isn't easy for anyone, risks exist and, in your work, the best way to learn is right before you. Let other people know that you are willing to tackle the most difficult tasks. And, when challenges present themselves, dive in and prove to yourself what you can do.

Sure you might end up with a few scars. But just remember, the easy path has never led to happiness.

TWENTY-FOUR

Ω

Stay Close To Your Best People

A client of mine called to say that his best employee, the only person capable of running his business, had just resigned. And, nothing he had said so far had changed the man's mind.

My reply, *"Nobody owns anyone and good people are free to leave. Did you ask him why he was leaving?"*

After a long pause my client replied, *"I asked and I heard what he said. But, it doesn't make sense to me. I had big plans for him."*

—*Dick Warn*—

And my reply, *"How long has been since you sat down with this man, asked about his family, his plans and any changes he would like to see in your firm?"*

His face delivered his answer. He had fallen into a very common trap. In most large organizations independent, hard-working employees carry the load, while managers take them for granted.

In most typical organizations, all of management's time and attention is invested in the slackers, hackers, and the living dead.

If you have employees, and you want to keep the very best, you have got to find ways to remain very close to them.

Good employees are a firm's most valuable assets.

TWENTY-FIVE

Ω

At-Bats, Hits, and Misses

Attempting to explain ways to live to his son, a father said, "Life is like baseball. It is a game of at-bats, swings, hits, misses, and home runs.

"The at-bats are your opportunities to try something new, to meet a stranger, or to help someone in need.

"The swings occur when you step forward and take your chances. And the hits occur when you connect with something and it feels good.

—*Dick Warn*—

"The misses occur when you don't connect. And the home runs occur when you discover a talent, find a friend, or discover something you love to do.

"To find happiness and feel good about yourself, you've got to step forward, take your swings, experience your misses and learn to get your hits. In no other way can you truly connect with life.

"True, your misses will out number the hits, but that doesn't matter. It's the same for everyone. So count your hits and forget your misses—playing the game with all you've got."

TWENTY-SIX

Ω

Worry and Stress—A Nation's Killers

Worry wears people down and drives them to make poor decisions. Factories, hospitals and rest homes are overflowing with people who should be living, yet they're dying. Stress, worry and depression have taken over their lives.

Stress, worry and depression are not *"out there."* These three are mental monsters eating away at people's will to live. And, the error so many people make is in ignoring a timeless principle: *Take no concern for tomorrow.*

—Dick Warn—

Thomas Carlyle, Scottish philosopher, said, *"Our main business is not to see what lies dimly at a distance, but to do what lies clearly at hand."*

And Peter Drucker, American-Austrian management consultant, said: *"Beyond the scope of managing ourselves for one day, everything else is a piece of cake."*

When we refuse to take charge of our own thoughts and allow worries to take over, we willingly become victims of circumstance, shipwrecked by indecision.

Dig in your heels and make up your mind to live one day at a time, leaving worry behind.

Worry and stress are proven killers.

TWENTY-SEVEN

Ω

Putting Our World Together

In his famous program *"Lead the Field,"* Earl Nightingale shares a story that everyone should be aware of.

The father of a five-year-old was attempting to watch a baseball game on television and his young son was running around wanting to play.

In an effort to slow his son down, the father cut a full-page ad from the newspaper that showed planet Earth as seen from space. He then tore the page into a dozen pieces and handed those pieces plus a roll of

—*Dick Warn*—

cellophane tape to his son, saying, *"Show me how fast you can put the world back together in perfect order."*

The son raced to his room, the father returned to the game, yet within minutes, the child returned with the world perfectly taped together.

The startled father asked, *"How did you do that so fast?"*

And the smiling child replied, *"On the back side of the world there was a picture of a man. I just taped the man together and the world came together."*

Following a long pause, the father replied, *"You're right, son. When a man is together, his world is together."*

TWENTY-EIGHT

Ω

Follow-Through

Having lunch with a highly respected building contractor, I asked, *"When selecting vendors, lenders, and subcontractors, what do you look for?"*

"The first thing I look for is honesty," the contractor said. *"My business is more than sticks and stones. Construction is the art of scheduling projects, just like a stage play. Each task, when completed, sets the stage for something else. When someone over-commits, under-delivers, or in any other way fibs it costs us money.*

—*Dick Warn*—

"The second thing I look for involves clear communication. I ask myself, are these people easy to reach? Do they return phone calls in a timely manner? And, in case of an emergency, can I find someone who cares after hours?

"The last thing I look for is their follow-through. Do they say what they mean, mean what they say, and honor their commitments?

"I have a quote on my wall that was written by F. W. Nichol. It says, 'When you get right down to the root of the meaning of the word "succeed," you find that it simply means to follow through.'

"For me, follow-through is the most important thing."

TWENTY-NINE

Ω

Less Stressful Living

Hans Selye, Canadian physician who researched stress, said, *"Mental tensions, frustrations, insecurity and aimlessness are among the most damaging stressors, and psychosomatic studies have shown how often they cause migraine headaches, peptic ulcers, heart attacks, hypertension, mental disease, suicide, or just hopeless unhappiness."*

Hopeless unhappiness, like cancer cells, slowly eats away our passion for living. Indian-born British author, Salman Rushdie, said, *"In this world without quiet corners, there can be no easy escapes from history, from hullabaloo, from terrible, unquiet fuss."*

—Dick Warn—

The fuss people make over movie stars, leaders and misguided politicians is wasted energy, contributing nothing to our world except worrisome noise. To achieve a more peaceful state of being, invest in Quiet Time—small slices of time used to re-center your mind on positive principles.

Peaceful souls who do this best build periods of Quiet Time into their daily schedules.

As Lily Tomlin, American comedienne, said, *"For fast-acting relief, try slowing down."*

THIRTY

Ω

Ten Two-Letter Words

Do you remember hearing or reading, "*If it is to be— it is up to me*"?

These 10 two-letter words state a universal reality, as changeless as the law of gravity. Yet, out of the millions of people who have read or heard these words spoken, how many have understood what they mean?

It doesn't appear to me that everyone sees the big picture.

—*Dick Warn*—

To those complaining about their wages, we should say, *"Become a more valuable employee."*

To those complaining about a lack of education, we should say, "Public libraries are open and free classes are available to people willing to learn to read."

To those complaining that they don't have enough time to read or attend classes, we should say, "You have the same amount of time as everyone else. Time is not your problem. What gives you trouble is your priorities. You still believe in something for nothing, as if the tooth fairy were coming."

In most nations the ladders are up, people are free to climb and library doors are open. In most places, useful information is available to everyone.

All truly successful happy people are self-taught.
The real learning begins after school.

THIRTY-ONE

Ω

Persistent Endless Trying

During an interview once I was asked what the most vital key to my success had been. I thought of my habit of reading, my willingness to set goals, to look in the mirror and to hold myself accountable. Each had played a role, but none was really *THE* key.

I had dreamed of being an author since grade school. A deep desire like this is nature's way of telling us what we should try. Yet, my early attempts were so horrible that even my closest friends said I should try something else.

— *Dick Warn* —

Life has taught me, however, that dreams like mine don't die because of talent or timing. Recurring deep-seated dreams die because someone gives up. Many talk themselves out of trying before they even begin, while others retreat at the first sign of trouble. Everyone can find excuses for quitting.

Anyone who can create excuses has the creative ability to solve problems and build a better world for themselves. The *HOW*, however, can only be found through persistent endless trying.

THIRTY-TWO

Ω

What Words Will You Choose?

It has been said, and I tend to agree, that words have ripple effects, the same as pebbles dropped into water. As Mother Teresa once said, *"Kind words can be short and easy to speak, but their echoes are truly endless."*

Words alter lives by shifting views, both for the good and otherwise. And, one of the most rewarding things you can do for others is to cause them to see an improved view of themselves.

The fault-finders, critics and complainers may think they're helping to improve the world, but they're

— *Dick Warn* —

really not. To see people actually improve, you've got to inspire them by pointing out their strengths and what they are doing right.

Every day we touch people with e-mails, over the phone, and sometimes in person. With every touch we have an opportunity to brighten someone's view.

What words will you choose?

THIRTY-THREE

Ω

We *CAN* Reinvent Ourselves

We are born with the freedom of choice, and that freedom includes making conscious decisions to change our lives by improving ourselves.

One habit that kept me down was smoking two packs of cigarettes a day for 40 years, and another one was occasionally drinking way beyond reason. I knew that both of these habits weren't good for me, but I didn't believe I could quit.

—Dick Warn—

My addiction to nicotine was more powerful than my desire to drink. I recall putting on patches, then lighting up.

The magic moment that gave me the strength to walk away from each of these habits, one at a time, arrived the instant my deep-seated beliefs switch from *"can't"* to *"can."*

If you are stuck with something you know you should walk away from, find people who have already dealt with that same habit and listen to them.

We may travel on different paths, yet all potholes are the same.

Out of the ashes of our past, we can reinvent ourselves—once we believe we can.

—More Miracle Minutes—

THIRTY-FOUR

Ω

Having A Bird's-Eye View

One bright sunny day two bugs went strolling through a carpet, weaving their way through a jungle of threads. The leader, a know-it-all control-freak, had noticed blue thread woven with green, and red thread woven with orange. So he said to his friend, *"It must have been idiots who wove this rug together."*

Two pigeons flying past an open window saw the same rug and were tantalized by delicate weaving. The pigeons circled for another view and both agreed as they flew away that this rug was the most beautiful rug they had ever seen.

—Dick Warn—

When we are down in the trenches, working hard and doing our thing, it is very easy to lose sight of the much larger picture.

The next time you feel like condemning someone for what they've done, take a long walk before you say anything.

In every situation there are several views. Ours is only one.

Just because we think we're right doesn't make it so.

THIRTY-FIVE

Ω

Inch by Inch

Have you ever wondered, listening to Bach, Beethoven, or Mozart, how one individual could write such music? Or driven passed Mt. Rushmore and marveled at how those faces were carved?

It is amazing what can be done when we create a vision, add desire and have the courage to take that first step. First steps, however, are killers when fear takes over.

Who knows how high they can fly, what discoveries they can make or what services they can provide? No

—Dick Warn—

one! And, when they don't take that first step, they will always wonder what might have been.

There is no fail-safe way to truly live, so the next time you are thinking about something you truly want to do and fear tempts you to change your mind, recall what these two men have shared:

"Whatever the mind can conceive and believe—it can achieve."

Napoleon Hill

"Inch by inch, everything is a cinch."

Dr. Robert H. Schuller

THIRTY-SIX

Ω

The Price of Bad Advice

People have opinions and most are willing to share them, yet life-altering decisions should be explored in the same way diamond cutters view diamonds—from every angle. And remember, no person can lead you farther than they have gone themselves.

When seeking advice about something you want, find and listen to people who have already achieved it. When seeking advice about your health, listen to healthy people. When seeking advice about peace of mind, listen to peaceful people.

—Dick Warn—

No matter what your desires, there are people who have already solved the challenges involved and achieved what you want. Those people know the ropes and how to climb. Everyone else is still guessing.

When you apply guesses in hopes of achieving your dreams the results may cause you to believe that you cannot—when, in fact, you can.

The most common price people pay for bad advice is giving up when they shouldn't.

THIRTY-SEVEN

Ω

Is It Tiger's Talent—or Luck?

Recently, at lunch, two men seated at a table beside me were sharing their beliefs about Tiger Woods and what made him such a successful golfer.

The first man believed Tiger has special gifts, that talent is the reason for his success. The other man disagreed. He believed that other players are just as talented. What made the difference was Tiger's luck.

So which is it—talent, or luck?

—*Dick Warn*—

In a recent interview, Tiger Woods shared the reality behind his awesome games when he said, "Everything can always be better. This game is fluid. It's always changing, it's always evolving. I could always hit the ball better, chip better, putt better, and think better. You can be better tomorrow than you are today."

The keys to Tiger's many successes are found in those nine words he said, "*You can be better tomorrow than you are today.*"

What sets Tiger Woods apart from the crowd is not talent or luck. It is Tiger's continual efforts to improve.

THIRTY-EIGHT

Ω

The Substance-Abuse Lie

At a meeting of hard-core abusers and losers, a man in charge asked, *"By a show of hands, how many of you drink daily?"*

After several hands went up, he asked a second question, *"Why do you people choose to drink so often?"*

One man said he suffered from low self-esteem and that life wasn't going his way. Another man said his wife was the problem; she didn't listen to him. And a third man claimed that substance abuse was beyond his control because he had a disease.

—Dick Warn—

The disease angle is one way to see it. Yet, in 40 years of sitting with hard-core drinkers, I have never seen anyone attacked by a bottle. The word "disease" has come from treatment centers calculating potential profits.

Life has shown us that we are *NOT* all wired the same. Some people can control their drinking and others cannot. And, as AA and NA have clearly proven, sobriety can be achieved when (1) someone openly admits they have a problem; (2) that person honestly wants to stop using; and (3) they have been given enough reasons and proof to believe that they "*can*" become clean.

Why do I dislike the substance-abuse lie? When people believe it's a disease beyond their control, some of them don't even try to get clean.

How do I know? I am an alcoholic who has been clean for over seven years.

THIRTY-NINE

Ω

When a Leaf Falls

When a leaf falls, its relationship with the tree is broken forever—and there is no going back. The same thing occurs in our own relationships. In some cases we can come back, but that relationship—whatever it was—is never the same.

Is this good or bad? I believe it's good. Over time, people tend to take people for granted. Things that should be done are often ignored; trust bridges become tarnished, and relationships get stuck.

Last week a client called to terminate a stuck relationship. I had been feeling frustrated with him,

—Dick Warn—

he was frustrated with me, and we were not working together. Once the initial shock wore off, I knew my client had done the right thing.

Our universe is strongly biased in favor of growth and forward motion. We are here to learn, to grow and to help each other.

Other than love, the strongest glues binding people together are trust and growth. When either of these is gone, it is time to move on.

FORTY

Ω

A Pivotal Key

When Abraham Lincoln said, *"A person will be as happy as they make up their minds to be,"* his four words, *"make up their minds,"* give us a pivotal key.

Most of my life I have said, *"If only I had more money I would be happy."* Yet, when I had more money I didn't feel any better. Happiness cannot be bought, nor can someone else make us happy. Happiness is a state of mind driven by the attitudes and reactions we choose.

Most people fail to choose. Rather than make up their mind and select their own thoughts, they wish

—Dick Warn—

things were different while allowing the opinions of others to control their life.

Everyone is free to take charge of their thoughts and select their beliefs. The brave souls who know this rise early, open books and work on their beliefs before they ever leave home.

A well-centered mind—focused on universal truths—is like wearing armor. It protects us from a continual barrage of negative garbage.

To paraphrase Abraham Lincoln, happiness results from our choices.

—More Miracle Minutes—

FORTY-ONE

Ω

Who Do You Hang With?

People can be found in three basic flavors: the Self-Starters, Kick-Starters and the Living Dead. When you aren't careful about the people you spend time with, it can be damaging.

The Living Dead can drag you down. The Kick-Starters are better to be with, but most of them are still wondering, wandering and guessing. The guessing can get you in trouble.

If you want to go beyond where you are, spend time with the Self-Starters. These people have fire in their

—Dick Warn—

bellies, hope in their hearts, and they are willing to help you. How can you spot them? They'll have light in their eyes.

Eyes are the window of the soul. When light is present it proves that they're truly alive and they've begun to apply some of the keys to a successful life.

So what are the keys? One of the most important keys is realizing that we must help other people get what they want, before we can get what we want. It's that old karma thing.

Begin looking for people with light in their eyes. Their presence will be uplifting and their advice empowering.

Start looking right now. Time doesn't wait.

—More Miracle Minutes—

FORTY-TWO

Ω

Trust Your Intuitive Feelings

One common thread running through the lives of highly creative people—the leaders, teachers, artists, architects, engineers and inventors making a difference—is that they have learned to trust their intuitive feelings.

In a hiring situation, I remember an applicant who tested well, responded with the right answers and had excellent references. Yet, something didn't feel right.

—Dick Warn—

Unable to explain what I felt, I hired the man. When we turned him loose he took credit for things he hadn't done, lied about what he was doing and left a trail of uncompleted tasks.

Our best guess, his glowing references had come from people who really wanted him gone.

We were born with an intuitive response system. This silent feeling that we often get comes from a cosmic guidance system. When we follow it, we are led in the right direction. When we ignore it, we set ourselves up for painful lessons.

Learning to trust this sixth sense that you already have is one of the most beneficial things you can ever do.

If you haven't been listening to your gut hunches, give it a try.

FORTY-THREE

Ω

Fight-or-Flight Response

In yesterday's local paper, a letter to the editor claimed that we, the United States of America, should pull out of Iraq and bring our troops home where it is safe.

Was it "safe" on September 11, 2001? Is it any safer now? There are several thousand angry misguided souls who believe they are serving a higher power by blowing themselves and others up.

The battles being fought are not over oil. They are being caused by ignorance and evil. As long as

—Dick Warn—

people in the world believe they can achieve their happiness by killing human beings, who is safe anywhere?

Our soldiers in Iraq are fighting the most difficult war our nation has ever fought, because the enemy blends in with everyone else and uses children to carry bombs. We are not talking about rational human beings. We are talking about people trained to kill in the name of a god that doesn't exist.

If we, the people who value life, don't deal with the insanity *"over there,"* it will soon be everywhere.

FORTY-FOUR

Ω

Three Myths About Success

First myth: *Hard work matters.* Most people believe if they work really hard, everything will eventually fall into place. That doesn't happen. What matters is working smart.

Second myth: *Money is the answer.* If that were true, all rich people would be happy. The truth is, true love, self-worth, peace of mind, and happiness cannot be bought no matter how many toys you have.

—Dick Warn—

Third myth: *Happiness is somewhere down the road.* With that distorted distant view, people miss what they could have had while worrying about where they're going.

To achieve happiness we must learn to live each day as it arrives and play the hand we have to play.

If we want more money, we must find ways to be of greater service to others.

If we want more love, we must find ways to be more loving.

Success and happiness are not *"where"* we are, but *"who"* we are, and how we've learned to play the game.

FORTY-FIVE

Ω

Three Myths About Money

First myth: *Money is evil.* Money is a power, the same as electricity, and money can be used for both good and evil. What determines its value is how it is used. And, you can help more people with it than without it.

Second myth: *Earnings determine a worker's value.* On each rung of an organizational ladder, some workers are paid far more than they are worth and others are paid far less. Yet the greatest value a worker can take away from their work is not in what they earn, but in what they learn.

—*Dick Warn*—

Third myth: *Go for the money.* When selecting where they will work, many people go for the money. That decision often leads people to hating their work.

To become the best we can be we need to be involved with things we believe in, aiming for dreams we're willing to work toward. This doesn't mean we have to love what we're doing every day. Some work is a means to an end. What we need to love is our objective.

No matter what you are doing to earn a living you are selling your time, talent and expertise to someone. Think of yourself as an independent contractor who has the freedom to increase earnings by increasing the value of what you're offering.

The key to earning more is outgrowing the position or situation you're in.

FORTY-SIX

Ω

What It Means to Be Truly Alive

Hurricanes Rita and Katrina, like other major disasters, draw the best out of some people, the worst out of others, and result in thousands of sound bites and pictures the media can use. What, however, deserves the most coverage?

It is not the looters, shooters, and angry people we should remember. It is the unsung heroes of every race and creed, from every state and some foreign countries, who placed service above self, leaving their families, homes and jobs to help others.

— *Dick Warn* —

If all the sound bites, pictures and facts were gathered together, it would be easy to see that the acts of compassion outnumbered the acts of insanity a thousand to one. Yet, what images do most people remember?

It would be nice if every place of employment and every public place where people gather had a picture of one unsung hero hanging on the wall. We need to be reminded of the thousands of people who left the warm comforts of their own homes to help strangers in need.

It isn't the looters and shooters that should be remembered, it is the people who value life and have compassion for others. Those are the ones who prove what it means to be truly alive.

—More Miracle Minutes—

FORTY-SEVEN

Ω

Making Enough Changes?

If change were easy, more people would have their lives together, and truly happy people would be easier to find.

Have you noticed when you ask, *"How are you doing?"* the number of people who try to hide reality? True happiness is a state of being that cannot be faked. Either a person has it or they don't. And, one non-optional aspect of true happiness is the willingness to change.

Most New Year's resolutions have very short life spans because of the effort it takes to change. Most people want the benefit of change without actually changing themselves.

Nolan Ryan, American baseball player, said, *"Enjoying success requires the ability to adapt. Only by being open to change will you have a true opportunity to get the most from your talent."*

Everyone has talents. Mastering life is nothing more than moving forward by finding better ways and making changes.

As you think about your life and where you are going, please consider these words from Karen Kaiser Clark, *"Life is change. Growth is optional. Choose wisely."*

— More Miracle Minutes —

FORTY-EIGHT

Ω

Fran Tarkenton Said

NFL quarterback, Fran Tarkenton, said, *"If football taught me anything about life and business, it taught me that you win the game one play at a time."*

The game of life, just like football, cannot be won with one big play. What governs winning is the attitude we bring to each situation and the choices we make. Listen intently, or totally ignore what you hear. Get involved, or silently retreat. Do the right thing, or do otherwise.

—*Dick Warn*—

People who learn to choose wisely eventually get what they want, while losers end up hating what they have and stand firm on their excuses.

Life is a work in process, and before any wise decisions can be made you must know what it is you want. Once you know what you want you can learn from other people who have already achieved the very same thing. They are the examples that we should be following.

Like a spider weaving a web, the very fabric of your life is woven by decisions. Choose wisely, my friend. Life doesn't wait for anyone.

FORTY-NINE

Ω

Earl Nightingale's Strangest Secret

After 30 years of research into the primary causes of success and failure, Earl Nightingale summed it up simply when he said, *"We become what we think about."*

Thoughts are not meaningless things. Every thought you hold has power, and what some people never see is how their negative thoughts drag them down.

Our mind is like a $10-billion computer that stores everything we say to ourselves about ourselves. Our "self-talk" programs our views and alters our reality.

—Dick Warn—

The next time you catch yourself saying things like, *"I just can't remember names"* or *"I'll never be able to learn that,"* halt that train of thought. Consciously switch to more positive affirmations, such as, *"Every day, in every way, I am getting better and better"* or *"I don't know now, but I can learn."*

Self-talk isn't optional.

Anyone who claims that their life sucks is really the true suckee, sabotaging their own self-worth.

Please don't be one of them.

—More Miracle Minutes—

FIFTY

Ω

Two Signs of Meaningful Maturity

In the beginning, back when our journey through life began, we were faced with an endless sea of options.

The problem with options it that we are biased toward the things we like and, at an early age, it is easy to assume that life is a happy meal with toys tossed in.

One of the first signs of maturity is realizing that there is more to life than toys and games, and that we cannot have our own way every day.

—*Dick Warn*—

Another sign of maturity is realizing that we alone are responsible for our own happiness, that the quality of our life depends on our choices, and that every decision we make has a consequence.

Putting off a decision may appear smart, yet "no" decision is still a decision—a decision to allow circumstances to rule. And, most of the time, a wrong decision is better than no decision, because we can always change our mind.

What we cannot do is reclaim the time wasted sitting, stewing and wondering. As Dwight D. Eisenhower, 34th President of the United States, said, *"The history of free men is never written by chance, but by choice; their choice."*

Work to become an effective decision-maker. You can do it if you want to.

—More Miracle Minutes—

FIFTY-ONE

Ω

The Keys to Getting

A free ride doesn't exist, the tooth fairy is a myth and, if hard work were the correct answer, most people would already have everything they want.

Truth is, too many people are standing at the wood stove of life crying, "Give me heat, and then I'll put in some wood."

In a book many people own, few read, and far less understand, we can find, "As ye sow, so shall you reap." This idea is not optional. Nor is it something

—Dick Warn—

we should review with attorneys. It is an absolute law, called "The Law of Service and Reward."

If you want more money, you must find ways to be of greater service to others.

If you want more happiness, you must find ways to help other people become happier. If you want more love, you must find ways to be more loving.

Just as there are no exceptions to the law of gravity, no one is an exception to the Law of Service and Reward. There are times when people believe they've gotten something for nothing, but time has a way of proving otherwise.

If you don't believe what I've just said about giving, try wearing a warm smile attached to a helping hand and see what happens.

What we give is what we get back.

FIFTY-TWO

Ω

Harry S. Truman Said

Harry S. Truman, 33rd President of the United States, once said, *"I never gave anybody hell! I just told the truth, and they thought it was hell."*

Hell occurs when lives are threatened, people are scared and foundations are crumbling.

What is weakening our nation? Conditional honesty, situational ethics, biased media and allowing special-interest groups to rewrite the rules.

—*Dick Warn*—

One of the most valuable guides ever written was written for West Point almost 100 years ago. The West Point Code of Ethics is short, simple, clear and concise: "I will not lie, cheat, or steal, nor tolerate those who do."

This universe that we all share is governed by a much higher order than special interests and personal desires.

Isn't it time that we, the people of this great world, say to ourselves, *"Enough is enough with the smoke and mirrors and the back-office games?"*

President Truman knew what he stood for, and so should we.

For the sake of our children, our grandchildren, and all others who follow, let us set the needed examples by applying—*"I will not lie, cheat, or steal, nor tolerate those who do"*—to our own lives.

Ω

Closing Comments

I thank you for being a reader. I thank you for being a thinker. And, I hope that you have been touched by something in this book.

If you know of someone else who has a mind and uses it, yet they have not discovered the benefits of reading, please loan them this book.

Not all sharp-minded "non-readers" will accept the challenge, but I have converted a few, and so can you.

Every time a non-reader is inspired to read and they gain life altering insights, who knows how far and wide improvements will spread. It's like dropping a pebble into a pond.

R. S. (Dick) Warn
Tualatin, Oregon USA

—Dick Warn—

— *More Miracle Minutes* —

Ω

More about Dick Warn

In 1978, Dick Warn formed Richard S. Warn & Associates to help business owners, managers and leaders achieve greater success in sales, management, and team building.

He has written and delivered over 800 custom workshops, 2,000 keynote speeches, and the audio versions of these Miracle Minutes can be heard on KTDD-AM (Riverside, California) and KMYT-FM (Temecula, California). You can hear samples by visiting: www.TheMiracleMinute.com.

For the past 27 years, Dick Warn has been invited back to deliver the opening keynote speeches at the Association of Washington Business' Business Week summer programs. Week-long programs sharing with high school students the principles of free enterprise, insights from business leaders, and the skills required for team building. Additional insights available at: www.wbw.org.

—Dick Warn—

In 1984, while working at The Salvation Army Adult Rehabilitation Center in Pasco, Washington, Dick began to focus on the connections between success in business and a successful life. His work with people at the center clarified the unbreakable bonds between the two. His own struggles with alcohol strengthened his resolve to help others by sharing what he has discovered.

Dick Warn is an author, speaker, consultant, coach and friend.

For additional insights into his life and career, please visit: www.TheMiracleMinute.com.

If you have any thoughts you want to share, please send them to: DickWarn@TheMiracleMinute.com.

ISBN 1425127649